SandCastle™

First Rhymes

Chuck Has a Big Truck

Anders Hanson

Consulting Editor, Diane Craig, M.A./Reading Specialist

ABDO Publishing Company

Published by ABDO Publishing Company, 4940 Viking Drive, Edina, Minnesota 55435.

Printed in the United States.

Credits
Edited by: Pam Price
Curriculum Coordinator: Nancy Tuminelly
Cover and Interior Design and Production: Mighty Media
Photo Credits: AbleStock, Digital Vision, Eyewire Images, Hemera, Photodisc

Library of Congress Cataloging-in-Publication Data

Hanson, Anders, 1980-
    Chuck has a big truck / Anders Hanson.
        p. cm. -- (First rhymes)
    ISBN 1-59679-463-1 (hardcover)
    ISBN 1-59679-464-X (paperback)
        1. English language--Rhyme--Juvenile literature. I. Title. II. Series.
PE1517.H345 2006
808.1--dc22
                                                                            2005044262

SandCastle™ books are created by a professional team of educators, reading specialists, and content developers around five essential components that include phonemic awareness, phonics, vocabulary, text comprehension, and fluency. All books are written, reviewed, and leveled for guided reading and early intervention reading, and designed for use in shared, guided, and independent reading and writing activities to support a balanced approach to literacy instruction.

Let Us Know

After reading the book, SandCastle would like you to tell us your stories about reading. What is your favorite page? Was there something hard that you needed help with? Share the ups and downs of learning to read. We want to hear from you! To get posted on the ABDO Publishing Company Web site, send us e-mail at:

sandcastle@abdopub.com

SandCastle Level: Beginning

-uck

buck

duck

muck

puck

truck

Look at the .

I see the   .

Look at the .

This is a .

I see a .

A buck is a dollar.

The duck is white.

The muck is brown.

The puck is hard.

The truck is purple.

Chuck Has a Big Truck

Chuck has a big truck.

Chuck is in his truck
when he sees a duck.

18

The duck that Chuck
sees from his truck
is stuck in the muck.

The duck
looks at Chuck
in his truck and says,
"Do you see my puck
in this muck?"

Chuck says,
"Yuck, duck.
For only a buck,
I'll use my truck
to get you
and your puck
out of the muck!"

About SandCastle™

A professional team of educators, reading specialists, and content developers created the SandCastle™ series to support young readers as they develop reading skills and strategies and increase their general knowledge. The SandCastle™ series has four levels that correspond to early literacy development in young children. The levels are provided to help teachers and parents select the appropriate books for young readers.

Emerging Readers
(no flags)

Beginning Readers
(1 flag)

Transitional Readers
(2 flags)

Fluent Readers
(3 flags)

These levels are meant only as a guide. All levels are subject to change.

To see a complete list of SandCastle™ books and other nonfiction titles from ABDO Publishing Company, visit www.abdopub.com or contact us at:
4940 Viking Drive, Edina, Minnesota 55435 • 1-800-800-1312 • fax: 1-952-831-1632